Eva & Maxime
THE BAYEUX
TAPESTRY
AND ITS MYSTERIES

Aurélie Derreumaux
Illustrated by José Mauduit
Inspired by an original idea by
Aurélie Derreumaux and Laurent Granier

OREP
EDITIONS

Eva and Maxime were in Bayeux, dressed up as a princess and a knight for the medieval fair.

'Hey,' a lady said as she passed by, 'are you pretending to be William the Conqueror and Queen Matilda?'

'Who is William the Conqueror?' Maxime wondered.

'William was the Duke of Normandy and he even became King of England! The story of his conquest is told on the Bayeux Tapestry.'

'And that's exactly what we're going to see!' their mum added.

'Would you like me to tell you the story? It's fascinating!'

'Oh, yes please!'

Did you know?

Every year, around 500,000 visitors come to admire the Tapestry! For this masterpiece is famous the world over!

A few minutes later, Eva and Maxime were in front of the Tapestry,

'Wow!' Maxime exclaimed. 'It's huge!'

'So, what story does it tell?' Eva asked.

'It illustrates a great battle, the Battle of Hastings, waged against the English army, and it explains how William became King of England in 1066. Look carefully, for every scene shows us an important event.'

Did you know?

The Tapestry measures around 68.5 metres in length, for a height of 50 centimetres. With its 58 scenes, it is said to be one of the very first comic strips ever created! It was produced from 1066 to 1082, so it is over 950 years old!

And the lady started to explain, *'It all began a long long time ago, in 1064. Edward the Confessor was the King of England and, since he was growing old, he needed to consider his succession. Who would be the next king?'*

Eva and Maxime's curious eyes and ears were wide open.

'Edward was married to Queen Edith, but they had no children. So he chose William to become king after his death, and he asked his brother-in-law, Harold Godwinson, to go and inform the Norman duke.'

Did you know?

A king's power is handed down from father to son. However, this king had no direct heir, in other words, no child to succeed him. So, he was allowed to choose another person to become the new king.

'But Harold's mission proved to be far more complicated and dangerous than expected!' the lady continued.

'Imagine... After a long journey, Harold finally arrived in France. Unfortunately, he did not land in Normandy, but further north on the Count of Ponthieu's land! Very quickly, he was taken prisoner.'

Did you know?

The Tapestry is believed to have been produced for the new cathedral in Bayeux, upon the Bishop Odo, William the Conqueror's brother's request.

'William had Harold released by paying a ransom, a huge sum of money.'

'But, how did he know he had been captured? asked Eva.

'William had spies who kept him informed of absolutely everything! Look at the tapestry. Can you see that man hiding behind a column? He was probably one of the duke's spies. Then William invited Harold to his palace in Rouen. It was at this point in time that Harold told William that King Edward had chosen him as his heir.'

Did you know?

How can we distinguish the English from the Normans on the Tapestry?
The English have moustaches and long hair, whereas the Normans have the back of their necks shaved. An interesting detail!

'Then William and his men set off on an expedition to Brittany.

'Why?' Maxime wondered.

'The Lord of Dol had rebelled against his chief, Conan, and had asked for William's help. As they crossed the Mont-Saint-Michel bay, the men found themselves trapped in the sinking sand! Summing up all his courage, Harold successfully saved several men! Finally, they waged battle in Dol, then in Rennes and Dinan, where Conan admitted defeat.'

Did you know?

The Tapestry offers us precious information on the period's clothes, castles, ships, etc. It also includes fabulous evidence of how people lived, in Normandy and in England, in the 11th century!

'To congratulate him for his bravery, William had Harold knighted and Harold promised to allow William to become king. He then returned to England to tell Edward of his travels.

'Is that Edward we can see lying down?' Eva enquired.

'Yes indeed! The king was very ill. That is why he quickly needed to choose an heir. However, things did not go according to plan...'

Did you know?

According to a legend, the Tapestry was produced by Queen Matilda - this is why it is also called 'Queen Matilda's Tapestry'. In fact, no one really knows exactly by whom or where it was made.

'Upon Edward's death, Harold broke his promise and, personally, became King of England.'

'But, that's betrayal!' Maxime cried in outrage.

'It was very difficult to resist the temptation, for, in doing so, Harold became very powerful... As the kingdom celebrated its new king, it is said that a comet flew through the sky, as a bad omen.'

Did you know?

The illustrations on the Tapestry's upper and lower border mainly represent familiar or fantasy animals. You can even spot a crow and a fox, the characters of the famous Aesop's fable, later related by Jean de la Fontaine!

'William then put together a plan to go to war and to recover the throne.'

'But, he'd need to cross the English Channel!' Eva exclaimed.

'Absolutely! When the time came to set sail, they boarded food, weapons and even horses! And they crossed by night. William was also on board - you can see him here.'

'Oh!' Maxime cried. *The boats look like Viking longboats!'*

'Exactly! That proves the Vikings' great influence in Normandy...'

Did you know?

It took William three months to gather together his men, to requisition most of Normandy's boats, to build new ones and to wait for favourable winds so they could set sail!

'When William's men landed in England, they set up camp in Hastings: they built fortifications with watch towers and a ditch to ward off the enemy. They organised their daily life, cooking and preparing grand banquets... However, informed of their presence, the English army was approaching!'

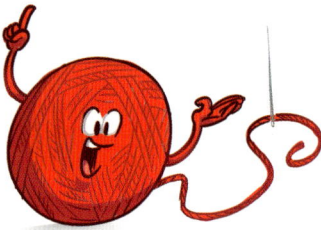

Did you know?

They call it a 'Tapestry', but it is, in fact, an embroidery. Each and every scene was hand-embroidered with woollen yarn, coloured using three plants: madder (red), weld (yellow) and woad (blue). By mixing these three colours, a total of 10 different hues was obtained!

'The Battle of Hastings took place on the 14th of October 1066, and it was a terrible one!'

'May nothing make you retreat, and may your hearts rejoice in victory!' William cried to his men to encourage them.

The English resisted and took shelter behind their shields... Until William tried a cunning tactic.

'What did he do?' Maxime asked.

'He pretended to flee with his men! And, in following them, Harold's army became scattered. William took advantage of their weakness to win the battle.

And this is where the Tapestry comes to an end,' the lady concluded.

Did you know?

At the time, the vast majority of the population was illiterate, in other words, very few people could read. The Tapestry is an exceptional work, for it enabled everyone to fully grasp the story.

'Harold was killed during the battle and William, Duke of Normandy, was crowned King of England on the 25th of December 1066!'

'Thank you very much, that was really interesting!' Eva said enthusiastically. 'Now I understand why they call him William the Conqueror!'

Eva and Maxime ran to meet their parents.

'En garde!' Maxime yelled. 'I am the new Duke of Normandy and King of England! 'May nothing make us retreat, and may our hearts rejoice in victory!'

Did you know?

DEX AÏE, *pronounced* Dayus Ayay *means 'God! Help us! This Norman war cry was both a call to God and a cry of encouragement.*

DID YOU KNOW?

The texts describing the scenes are in Latin, an old language used in written texts in the Middle Ages.

The Tapestry has travelled a great deal! Up to the end of the 18th century, it was kept as part of the Treasure of Bayeux Cathedral. In 1803, Napoleon Bonaparte had it taken to Paris in order to popularise his plan to invade England. During the Second World War, it was kept safe in the Château de Sources, near Le Mans, before being transferred to the Louvre in Paris. In 1944, it escaped being taken to Germany and, after the Liberation, it was finally brought back to Bayeux where it is still exhibited today.

The Tapestry is a listed historic monument since 1840 and is on the Unesco Memory of the World international register since 2007.

BAYEUX TAPESTRY –
TH CENTURY.
© BAYEUX TOWN COUNCIL.

BAYEUX MEDIEVAL FAIR. © BAYEUX TOWN COUNCIL.

BAYEUX TAPESTRY – 11TH CENTURY. © BAYEUX TOWN COUNCIL.

BAYEUX CATHEDRAL
© BAYEUX TOWN COUNCIL.

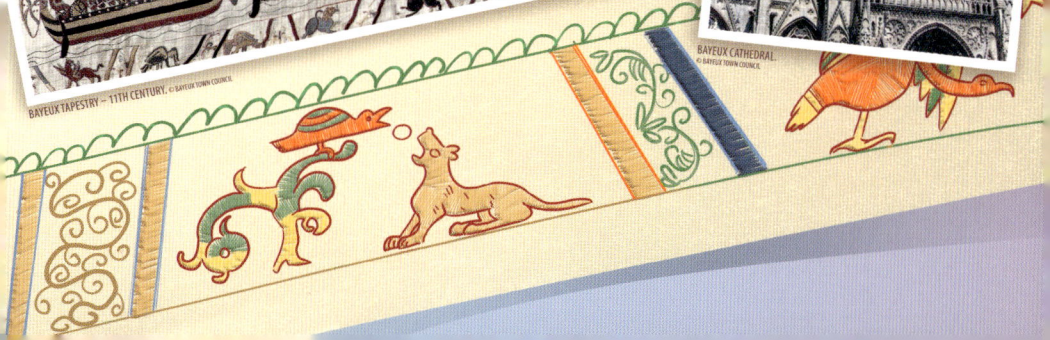

BAYEUX TAPESTRY – 11TH CENTURY. © BAYEUX TOWN COUNCIL.

Royal profiles

WILLIAM
THE CONQUEROR

Duke of Normandy since the age of 7 or 8 years, from 1035 to 1087. He was married to Matilda of Flanders. William was initially a vassal to the King of France, in other words he paid homage to him. However, by becoming King of England, he was even more powerful than the King of France! That's why, later French kings tried several times to conquer Normandy, finally succeeding in 1204.

EDWARD
THE CONFESSOR

He was King of England for 24 years, from 1042 to 1066. Following a Danish invasion, Edward was forced to flee England. Since his mother was the daughter of the Duke of Normandy Richard I, he sought refuge in Normandy where he remained for almost 30 years! This is when he met William. In 1042, Edward took the English throne and rallied round a number of Norman advisers, to counter the great power of the Godwin family, the most influential after that of the king. Since he had no children, and since he felt more of a Norman than an Englishman, Edward chose William as his heir.

HAROLD
GODWINSON

He was King Edward's brother-in-law and was England's last Anglo-Saxon king. Despite Edward's decision, he took the English throne on the 6th of January 1066, but he died during the Battle of Hastings against William's army on the 14th of October the same year.

Thanks:
We would like to extend our gratitude to Mme Sylvette Lemagnen, chief honorary curator of the Bayeux Tapestry, for her help and advice in compiling this work.